Orangutans

Patricia Kendell

Alligators   Chimpanzees   Dolphins   Elephants
Giraffes   Gorillas   Grizzly Bears   Hippos
Leopards   Lions   Orangutans   Pandas   Penguins
Polar Bears   Rhinos   Sea Otters   Sharks   Tigers

Published by Raintree, a division of Reed Elsevier, Inc.

Library of Congress Cataloging-in-Publication Data

Kendell, Patricia.
  Orangutans / Patricia Kendell.
    p. cm. -- (In the wild)
Summary: A simple introduction to the orangutan and its life in the rain forest.
Includes bibliographical references (p.   ).
  ISBN 0-7398-6636-2 (lib. bdg. : hardcover)
  1. Orangutan--Juvenile literature. [1. Orangutan.] I. Title. II. Series.
  QL737.P96 K35 2003
  599.88'3--dc21
                          2002152011

Printed in Hong Kong. Bound in the United States.

07 06 05 04
10 9 8 7 6 5 4 3 2 1

Photograph acknowledgments:
BBC Natural History Unit 1 & 22 (Anup Shah);
Bruce Coleman 9 (Alain Compost), 29 (Gerald S Cubitt),
11 (Fredriksson), 10 (Werner Layer), 20 (Jorg & Petra Wegner);
FLPA 19 (Minden Pictures), 18 (Jurgen & Christine Sohns);
HWPL/Orangutan Foundation 17, 26; Nature Picture Library
16 (Neil Lucas); OSF cover & 6 (Daniel Cox), 4, 7 (Mike Hill), 25
(Harold Taylor), 5, 8, 12, 14, 23, 27, 28 (Konrad Wothe);
SPL 15 (Renée Lynn); Still Pictures 21 & 32 (Compost/Visage),
13, 24 (Dario Novellino).

Contents

Where Orangutans Live

Orangutans live on the islands of Borneo and Sumatra near Asia.

They are the only members of the **great ape** family
that spend most of their time in the trees of the
rainforest. Orangutan means "person of the forest."

Baby Orangutans

When an orangutan is born, it is small and helpless like a human baby.

The baby orangutan will drink milk from
its mother until it is about three and a half
years old. Then it starts to eat other food.

Looking After the Baby

A baby orangutan stays close to
its mother, often riding on her back.

Orangutan mothers are very caring.
They protect their babies from danger and
groom them to make sure they stay clean.

Family Life

Mothers and babies stay together in small, friendly groups until the babies are big enough to live on their own.

Male orangutans live alone. They will fight with other males to keep control of their **territory** and the female orangutans who live there.

Learning and Playing

The young orangutans learn from their mothers how to behave and what foods to eat.

They play games with one another. This helps
them to grow strong. They get to know the
forest and they learn how to survive there.

Getting Around

Orangutans can swing through the trees by hooking their long, thin hands and feet over the branches.

When they are on the ground, orangutans walk using both their hands and feet.

Eating...

Orangutans eat mainly plant foods like fruit, leaves, bark, and flowers. They pick the food as they swing through the trees.

Orangutans are very fond of fruit. They use their
fingers and thumbs like we do to peel and eat it.

...and Drinking

Orangutans get most of their water by eating plants, by licking rainwater from leaves, or from their wet fur.

They also collect water from tree hollows
and rivers by scooping up the water and
licking their wet, hairy wrists.

Resting

Searching for food and eating it takes
up most of the orangutan's day.

Each night, an orangutan makes a leafy
nest high up in a tree to get settled in
for a well-earned sleep.

The Clever Orangutan

Like all of the great apes, orangutans are very intelligent. They can make tools from sticks to get food out of narrow spaces and to use for scratching their backs.

Some orangutans have also been taught to
communicate with people using **sign language**.

Threats...

Much of the orangutan's forest home is being destroyed. People cut down the trees and sell them, and then they plant new crops in their place.

In some places, oil palm trees are planted.
The oil from these palms can be sold to make
money. Farmers often shoot orangutans when
they catch them eating the young trees.

...and Dangers

Some baby orangutans are sold **illegally** as pets. Unfortunately, people cannot handle them when they grow up.

These orangutans are being helped by people
to learn how to live in the forest again. It is
difficult for the orangutans because they have
not learned how to find food for themselves.

Helping Orangutans to Survive

Instead of selling the baby orangutans for pets,
encouraging tourists to come to see wildlife is
a better way for local people to earn money.

Orangutans can live more safely in these
protected areas of forest. Here they have
enough space to find the food they need.

Further Information

Find out more about how we can help orangutans in the future.

ORGANIZATIONS TO CONTACT

World Wildlife Fund
1250 24th Street, N.W.
P.O. Box 97180
Washington, D.C. 20077-7180
http://www.wwf.org

Orangutan Foundation International
822 S. Wellesley Avenue
Los Angeles, CA 90049
http://www.orangutan.org

BOOKS

Grindley, Sally. *Little Sibu-An Orangutan Tale*. Atlanta, GA: Peachtree Publishing, 1999.

Sourd, Christine. *The Orangutan-Forest Acrobat*. Watertown, MA: Charlesbridge Publishing, 2001.

Taylor, Barbara. *Monkeys and Apes*. Columbus, OH: McGraw-Hill Children's Publishing, 2002.

Woods, Mae. *Orangutans*. Edina, MN: Abdo Publishing Company, 1998.

Glossary

WEBSITES

Most young children will need adult help when visiting websites. Those listed have child-friendly pages to bookmark.

http://www.rainforestlive.org.uk
Go to Kidz to find out about rainforests and why they should be saved.

http://www.geoimagery.com/publishers/King.html
The story, in pictures, of the rehabilitation of an orangutan called King.

great ape – (grayt ape) the animal family that includes chimpanzees, gorillas, bonobos, and orangutans.

groom – (groom) to clean fur by picking out dirt and insects.

illegally – (ill-LEE-gul-lee) against the law.

protected areas – (pruh-TEKT-ed AIR-ee-uhz) safe places where wild animals can live freely.

rainforest – (rayn-FOHR-usts) forests in hot, moist places.

sign language – (siyn LAYN-gwig) using hands and gestures to communicate instead of speech.

territory – (TER-uh-tor-ee) the home area of an animal.

Index